One Word Meditations

Scott Shaw

Buddha Rose Publications

One Word Meditations
Copyright © 2015 by Scott Shaw
All Rights Reserved

No part of this book may be reproduced in any manner without the expressed written permission of Scott Shaw or his representatives.

Rear cover photographs of Scott Shaw by Hae Won Shin. Copyright © 2015 All Rights Reserved.

First Edition 2015

Library of Congress: 2015933135
ISBN 10: 1-877792-82-9
ISBN 13: 9781877792823

Printed in the United States of America
10 9 8 7 6 5 4 3 2 1

For Paul Reps

One Word Meditations

Introduction:

Open to any page in this book, read the word and allow your mind to analyze what the word means to you.

yes

no

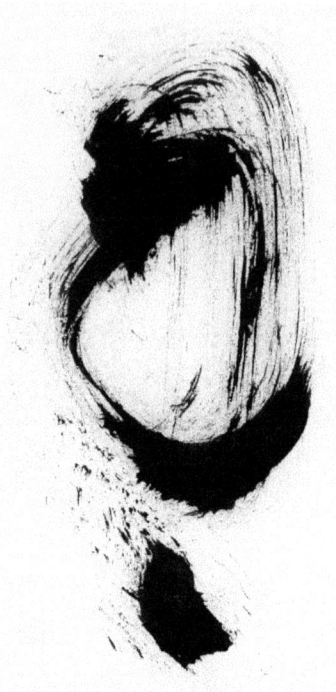

find

peace

listen

breathe

forever

love

silence

mind

surrender

forgive

forgotten

caution

wait

art

past

sit

patience

distance

displace

conceive

run

ambition

desire

lost

last

death

capture

expand

relax

function

contract

comply

rely

absolute

refrain

necessity

hate

divine

present

presence

before

after

never

now

beyond

sky

believe

space

abandon

caress

care

careful

lie

cause

truth

almost

heaven

hell

sanctuary

source

continue

hidden

anger

sealed

opportunity

live

disintegrate

erase

one

two

forget

hide

replace

abundance

dissolve

pretend

remember

conceal

bliss

god

exaggerate

essence

appeal

isolate

force

time

resolve

repeat

oblivion

energy

think

want

light

have

memory

lust

contemplate

addition

subtraction

worth

in

out

disguise

illumination

enlightenment

end

Scott Shaw Books-in-Print:

About Peace: A 108 Ways to Be At Peace

When Things Are Out of Control

Advanced Taekwondo

Arc Left from Istanbul

Ballet for a Funeral

Bangkok and the Nights of Drunken Stupor

Bangkok: Beyond the Buddha

Bus Ride(s)

Cairo: Before the Aftermath

Cambodian Refugees in Long Beach, California: The Definitive Study

Chi Kung For Beginners

China Deep

Echoes from Hell

Essence: The Zen of Everything

e.q.

Guangzhou: A Photographic Exploration

Hapkido: Articles on Self-Defense: Volume 1

Hapkido: Articles on Self-Defense: Volume 2

Hapkido: Essays on Self-Defense

Hapkido: The Korean Art of Self-Defense

Hong Kong: Out of Focus

Independent Filmmaking: Secrets of the Craft

In the Foreboding Shadows of Holiness

Israel in the Oblique

Junk: The Backstreets of Bangkok

*Last Will and Testament According to the
Divine Rites of the Drug Cocaine*

L.A.: Tales from the Suburban Side of Hell

Los Angeles Skidrow: 1983

*Marguerite Duras and Charles Bukowski:
The Yin and Yang of Modern Erotic Literature*

Mastering Health: The A to Z of Chi Kung

Nirvana in a Nutshell

On the Hard Edge of Hollywood

Pagan, Burma: Shadows of the Stupa

*Sake' in a Glass, Sushi with Your Fingers:
Fifteen Minutes in Tokyo*

Scream of the Buddha

Scream: Southeast Asia and the Dream

Scribbles on the Restroom Wall

Samurai Zen

Sedona: Realm of the Vortex

Shama Baba

Shanghai Whispers Shanghai Screams

Shattered Thoughts

Singaore: Off Center

South Korea in a Blur

Suicide Slowly

Taekwondo Basics

Ten to Thirty

The Chronicles: Zen Ramblings from the Internet

*The Ki Process: Korean Secrets for
Cultivating Dynamic Energy*

The Little Book of Yoga Breathing

The Little Book of Zen Mediation

The Lyrics

The Most Beautiful Woman in Shanghai

The Passionate Kiss of Illusion

The Screenplays

The Tao of Chi

The Tao of Self Defense

The Voodoo Buddha

*The Warrior is Silent:
Martial Arts and the Spiritual Path*

The Zen of Life, Lies, and Aberrant Reality

The Zen of Modern Life and the Reality of Reality

TKO: Lost Nights in Tokyo

*Urban India: Bombay, Delhi, Lucknow
Varanasi and Bodhi Gaya: Shade of the Bodhi Tree*

Wet Dreams and Placid Silence

Woods in the Wind

Yoga: A Spiritual Guidebook

Yosemite: End of the Winter

Zen and Modern Consciousness

Zen Buddhism: The Pathway to Nirvana

Zen Filmmaking

Zen in the Blink of an Eye

Zen Mind Life Thought

Zen O'clock: Time to Be
Zen: Tales from the Journey
Zero One

www.ingramcontent.com/pod-product-compliance
Lightning Source LLC
Chambersburg PA
CBHW061758110426
42742CB00012BB/1940